A Threshold We Carry

A Threshold We Carry

Poems by

Nick Trelstad

Cover design by Shay Culligan
Library of Congress Control Number: 2022944776

ISBN: 978-1-63980-204-3

Kelsay Books
502 South 1040 East, A-119
American Fork, Utah 84003
Kelsaybooks.com

Acknowledgments

Grateful acknowledgment is given to the editors of the following literary magazines and anthologies in which some of these poems, or earlier versions of them, first appeared:

Blue Marble Review: "Gray Wolf"

Bringing Joy: A Local Literary Anthology: "The Modern Wendigo"

Dillydoun Review: "Doe"

The Freshwater Review: "At Temperance Bay," "After Death"

Santa Clara Review: "Ringlorn," "I Said Your Name"

Scriblerus Review: "RSVP"

Red Weather Review: "Socrates Serves Me a Drink at Happy Hour," "Bear"

Special thanks as well to my beta readers: Ellie Larson, Nathan Larson, Mary Bergquist, and Eddy Simonson. Without your thoughtful suggestions and insights into the reader experience, this book could never have reached its full potential.

Many thanks to Madeline Hill for the wonderful cover design, and thanks again as well to Ellie Larson for the author photo too.

Contents

For my family, friends, and everyone at odds with the self.
Come forth into the light of things, let Nature be your teacher.
—William Wordsworth

The mass of men lead lives of quiet desperation.
—Henry David Thoreau

Bear

And in the north woods, when the snow has gone,
he paces slowly far and small those spaces at night,

black like a shadow of a shadow.
Over those dark fields of silence,

that long valley of solitude, he travels.
The wedge of his head, slung low

from muscular shoulders, sniffs the earth.
His tongue like a flame flicks above the grass

tasting the scent of blackberries and new birth
for which he hungers. He has no map, no compass,

direction is merely the way he walks, lumbering.
All night I lie awake thinking of him, his claws

cutting against the stone sides of the mountain
as he descends to the threshold of the city—

that tumor of light blazing upward
into the distances of the night.

At Temperance Bay

The full moon,
plump as a plum,
overflows.
Her pale light puddles
on the lake's surface,
like a stream it runs
to the shallows
where I stand
submerged
up to my knees
in the water.

Little waves lap
at the rocky shore—
rising, breaking,
falling back
into their own
emptiness
while I turn
to step back
into mine.

Salamanders

Beyond the willows
where the river bends,
beneath moss-covered rocks
and fallen branches,
deep in the mire,
damp and dark,
they have hidden

themselves among the dead
leaves in which they feed,
in which their toothless mouths
chirp—barely audible,
yet still musical.

When I was a child
I'd hunt the marshlands,
bucket in hand, clattering
through the swamp grass.

I'd choose the stones
and stump hollows,
reach forward
into the thick dampness;
my hands feeling blindly
for the thin, smooth bodies.

They too, blind
in the darkness,
sense me,
and again sound
their chirps—
soft, melodic,
as they move deeper
in the muck
away from reaching hands.

Where Have the Waters of Boyhood Gone?

The other neighborhood boys and I
would march in our pack
through the northern outback's
many mad sadnesses of youth.

Saturday mornings we'd go down
to the stone-cut quarry,
and dive from those upper bluffs
into the unblinking pupil ponds.
We'd jump, fall, cannonball
into that icy water—
our bodies consumed
by those dark depths
only to float back up.
Always to float back up.

Yes, what they say is true, boys
will be buoyant—will be thrown
to the murky waters of masculinity,
be expected to slide clear
across those waves like a dinghy
unzipping the surface, leaving
the world un-whole in their wake.

Gray Wolf

I find it laying
in the grass

beneath the shade
of a jack pine.

Red streaked saliva drips off
yellowed fangs and pale gums

while its chest pulls
in shallow breaths

rising and falling
like the restless boughs

above its body.
When I look down

into its hazel eyes
and unpleading pupils,

I know there is nothing
anyone could do.

Even still, I stand beside it.
I stop watching the blood

spill from its side. I close my eyes
and imagine its undeath.

The wolf sucks bloody saliva
back into its mouth.

It stands while pulped organs
and shattered bones reform.

The bullet spits from its side
and flies across the field—

back down a rifle's barrel.
The spent shell leaps back up

from the grass and glides
into the chamber

at the slide of a lever.
The casing remarries the bullet

when the hunter pulls the trigger.
He lowers the gun, locks

eyes with the wolf,
watches it walk

backward
into the woods.

After Death

A red sun climbs the pines,
branch over branch,

this first morning that I woke
and you did not.

I sit alone sipping coffee
at the window, across the room

your death bed lies
empty.

They had already come
to collect you, carry you away,

but left the bed sheets folded
open, as if anticipating a return.

Outside, the world begins
to remember itself—

I watch the darkness rise like ash
kicked up from the grass

as I try to make sense
of a world without you:

Will the mourning doves still
sing their shrill, heavy songs?

Will the postmen, like doctors,
still make their rounds?

The empty air of the house
offers no answer except

the hands of the clock
lurching forward

from now
into forever.

Swans

Two fly down from the north,
set their wings and glide
to a stop on the surface
of the Snake River. It is late
September now, and they have paused
on their long journey south.

While I watch them graze
on wild rice and watercress,
I can only wonder what it is
to see my world from above: the house
where I walk from room to room,
the fields and pines I've wandered
down and back through most of my life—
how small it all must be.

And though I know
their trumpetings to each other
are mere instinct, sharp calls
back and forth, I wonder if they discuss
what they've passed over:
the loneliness of cities
and the people they ensnare,
those who can't fly away
when the world goes frigid,
and so grow colder
in their rigid paths each year.

As they depart on wings
like white blades, they sing
the story of human isolation
until the suffering is nothing
but an abstract, and fades
below their sad, dark song.

RSVP

After they buried you, I found myself
in my bedroom thumbing through

a shoebox of card—searching in the baptisms,
birthdays, first communions, confirmations.

I found you between Christmas and Valentine's,
on a piece of parchment folded over and over

on itself in a small square. I pulled it open
and it unfurled into rivers of ink.

Every letter connected to the last, eddying over
and around each other in unbroken streams

still swirling toward the empty places
where words, like water, cease to start or end.

Bleeding through the cursive lines, you
speak the last note you ever sent me:

I am sorry I can't be there . . .
You begin.

Crows

One comes cawing
up from the trees—

then three, then seven.
Each bird rising

like a bit of night
broken loose

after a long sleep
spent dreaming

of the shape they want
their lives to take.

All night, huddled
among the cedar limbs,

they summoned
those deft, dark wings.

I Said Your Name

But I meant
the way oak leaves
ruddy and drop
like rust
from the sunset.

I meant
the creek's recital,
with its tumbles
and eddies, falling
into itself, echoing
from one year
into the next.

I said your name, but I meant
how snow becomes
the downward drift
of light, flake
after flake, upon the Earth
they buried you in.

Doe

And I have something to expiate: a pettiness.
—D.H Lawrence

From the window of my office
I watch her plump brown body
emerge from the underbrush—
carried on legs thin as saplings.
Hers is a gentle step too soft
to disturb the budless willow branches
frosted from the first snow.

And I, from my office, want nothing
but to step out those doors
and join her there beyond
that border only wild things can cross.
A threshold we carry in our lives
of which we know nothing.

As I watch her disappear just as quick
as she arrived—unexpected, unbound
back into the snow burdened boughs,
I too have something to expiate:
not a pettiness, but a longing.

Socrates Serves Me a Drink at Happy Hour

And, again, he explains that the beer
he has placed before me may not actually be beer—
that the frosted mug cooling my palm

may not be cold, may not be wet.
In fact, he states, *we can never be sure
you are holding anything at all.*

I try to follow his logic, musing
about the broken glass on the bar floor
that was once an empty bottle, and before that, filled.

I tell him I could cast off my loafers, and he his sandals,
walk barefoot across the glass shards, and why not?
We would never know if our feet felt pain,

if they actually bled.
Precisely, he says smiling behind the bar.
Outside, the sun is setting,

or at least it seems to be,
while men in dark suits emerge
from offices across the street,

from which they may
or may not be
returning home.

Fox

I had seen his prints
in the snow
before I saw him
at the meadow's edge,
tucked against the ground,
his shoulders tense as springs,
his head tilted, listening.

He is silent,
even as he leaps and dives,
even when his jaws glide shut.
There is nothing you can hear
but the wind ripping
through the juniper,
across the meadow,
into what lies beyond.

And later, when you find
only the holes in the snow
where he pounced, and the fallen tufts
of field mouse fur scattered, and red
splatters on the canvas of the Earth,

even then, you will hear nothing
but the north wind whistling
from one day into the next.

The Modern Wendigo

In the fruit bowl
on the table, an orange
is doing everything

except eating itself,
but the thin, shiny
flesh still begs

to be peeled.
Like now,
he is chewing

his fingernails
at the kitchen table
while she

sucks gleefully
at the small blood bubbles
on her pin-pricked fingertip.

That's not to say
we crave our own
consumption,

but there is an ache—
like the old gods
of famine who dwell

in our guts and
demand fresh
flesh and blood.

Like the eagle
on the side
of the road

feasting
on the still
warm carcass

of another eagle,
we are hungry
for ourselves.

Moose

Slowly my canoe drifts
down the river, swollen

from the spring thaw,
into marshlands no one owns.

There, from the bulrush
and spruce, he emerges—

his bone crown brimming green
with moss and algal bloom.

Here, in these boggy acres,
he is king of cattails and aspens,

and I am but an interloper—
I have merely passed into his realm.

The longing of my life is to float
awhile across slow moving waters,

to empty myself of everything
and learn what it is to be.

But, he stomps a hoof and grunts
his stern warning from the shallows,

and I know I must turn back, for he sees me
clearly: no wild thing, no singer of songs.

Meanwhile, all along the riverbanks,
the birches, restless in the April breeze,

unburden themselves of themselves:
leaf by golden leaf.

In a Field Near Jewett, Minnesota

I have been thinking of living
the way the wildflowers do,

though they rise and fall
with the changing winds,

and the roaming deer consume.
Though they have no homes—

no place to rest their heads,
no heads to place to rest.

Still, I would like to do it,
to leave the city, the stoplights

and shopping malls,
to do as the snow in spring

and wash myself
of myself.

And if I were an aster, I could wait
all day for the soft body

of the bumblebee to tumble
upon me with the breeze,

to take freely the pollen
that belongs to neither I nor it.

O Wind, great and ceaseless urger,
move your invisible vessel through me

as you pass through the field lilies.
Bear away what left I have to give

across these wide plains to the pines,
those living palaces of needles.

Ruffed Grouse

After I culled his body from the air
at the pull of a trigger, he thrashed

and flailed in his own sudden heaviness
and died among the green leaves

of clover he had feasted on.
Later, I took him home,

dressed his flesh from his hollow
bones, and ate him. Now, the forest

is in me: I am the grouse,
the thunder of his wings

drums in my chest; we are
enmeshed, inseparable—

both doomed to go below
that long, looming field

of milkweed and grain, to feed
those eager buds of clover.

For Every Action There Is an Equal, Opposite Reaction

For every bird,
there is a broken wing.

Every hyacinth,
a hemlock.

Every elation,
an overdose.

For every child loved,
there is one beaten,

bagged,
buried in the yard.

With every tragedy,
some twisted beauty.

Even the names
of the dead

read aloud
sound like a song.

Meadowlark

Each morning, she rises
from her nest along the river valley—

warbling and trilling as she comes.
And always, I find her there,

perched in the upper limbs of an oak
in a glade beyond the pines

serenading the sun as it crests
the horizon's endless sill.

Her song tells the oldest story
of life, death, and that long,

dark field that rises and falls
between them.

From where I lie below her,
in the dew damp grass,

I close my eyes and listen
to the rhythms of her meadow song

rising, twisting, sailing over
the threshold of the world.

Ringlorn

All of my childhood,
it had no name.

It crept through the Solana woods, swinging
willow branch to willow branch.

It slumbered in the mud with the frogs, waiting
to fill the spring air with throaty song.

It roosted in the rafters with barn swallows
and joined in their restless chattering.

It galloped in the pasture with the geldings,
and gnawed at the walls like a red squirrel.

It rose like fog above the thickets,
rusted with the haybine forgotten in the field,

drank from every stream,
ate wild plums and honeysuckle,

swam through the air with song birds
and sung in the long grass like a cricket.

At night, it hid in the cornfields,
dark and thick, and danced among the stalks—

who in their endless swaying whispered:
wild, wild, wild.

About the Author

Nick Trelstad is a poet and English teacher from northern Minnesota. He received his B.A. in English from The College of St. Scholastica in May of 2021 and has since gone on to have his works appear in a number of literary magazines, journals, and anthologies.

www.ingramcontent.com/pod-product-compliance
Lightning Source LLC
Chambersburg PA
CBHW030815090426
42737CB00010B/1291